AF576907

Through the Viewing Glass

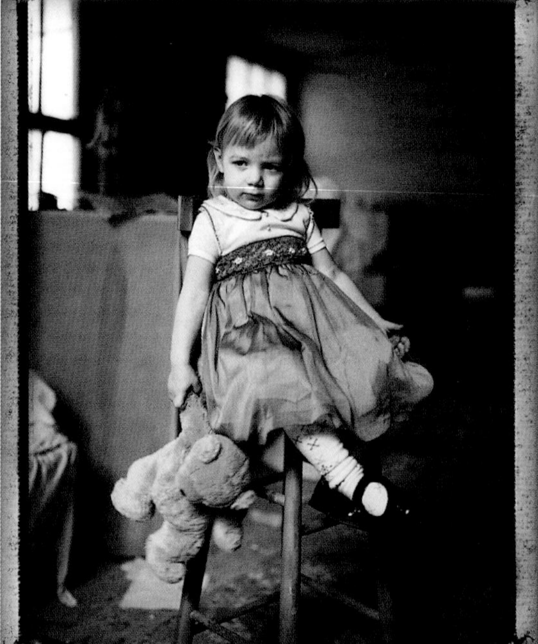

Through the Viewing Glass

Reflections on Photographing Children

By 3 D

ATRIA BOOKS

New York London Toronto Sydney

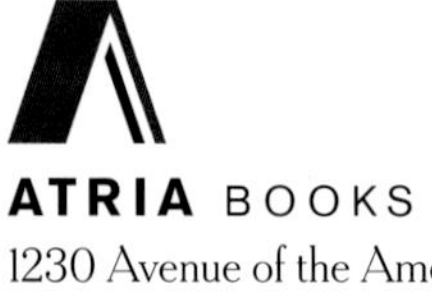

ATRIA BOOKS
1230 Avenue of the Americas
New York, NY 10020

ISBN: 0-7434-8358-8

First Atria Books hardcover edition May 2004

10 9 8 7 6 5 4 3 2 1

Manufactured in China

For information regarding special discounts for bulk purchases, please contact Simon & Schuster Special Sales at 1-800-456-6798 or business@simonandschuster.com

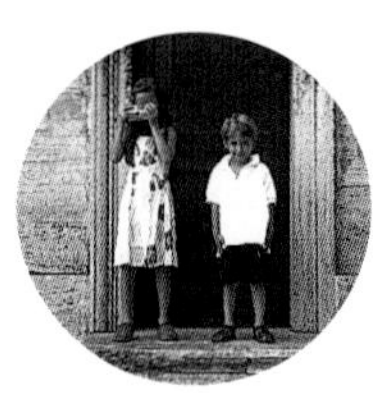

To Elly and Jesse,
without whom this book
would not exist—
and to others in our families
who helped us see
that it could.

Contents

The Camera *12*
Musings on the nature of the tool and its purpose

Jesse *20*
A child's take on being studied through the lens

The Photographer *72*
A shutterbug reflects on motives and methods

"Look up,
speak nicely,
and don't
twiddle your
fingers all
the time."

—Lewis Carroll,
Through the Looking Glass

WHY do we take so many pictures of our children?

It's as if we want to document every nanosecond of their lives. We dutifully record them eating, sleeping, waking, bathing; with friends; alone; dressed up; undressed. In the face of relentless change, we yearn for a way to preserve every moment. With the photograph, we think we can make time stand still. Our images are a reflection of the past and an archive for the future.

We use our photos to tell our stories. As proud parents, we want to show off our children; to share them with others. Pictures can be the quick fix that keeps fading relationships alive—a reminder to distant family and friends that we are still around. We send pictures we have taken in place of letters we have not written.

As photographers, we try to save an emotional memory with a visual medium. Most of our photographs portray scenes of family bliss: of children well behaved and parents well loved. The ideal, not necessarily the real. We say we want to remember each and every thing, but do we?

What we choose to photograph—or not photograph—helps us in our need for convenient forgetfulness. The perimeter of our four-sided picture frames only a small slice of life, leaving out more complex and sometimes less desirable content. We create myths with our pictures, and in time these myths are the only remnants of the experience.

Whoever said that a picture never lies must never have taken one. Even when photographs seem to be an accurate means of expression and communication, they are not entirely truthful. In photography, there are no absolutes.

The three sections of this book present three different perspectives on the photograph: those of the camera, the child-subject, and the parent-photographer. While each conveys one side of the story, it is the printed image that in the end becomes the shared history.

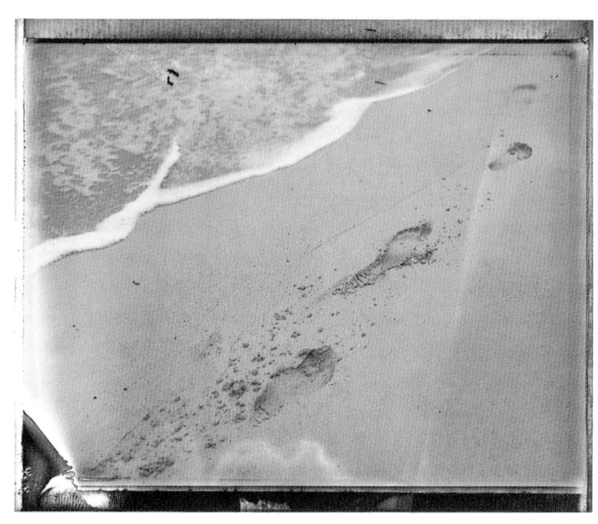

The Camera

camera (kam´ərə)

(noun): an eye; box with a hole; memory device; time machine; (verb): mirror, pursue, subjugate; capture; (adj.): crafty; selective; remorseless.

"Well, now that we have seen each other," said the Unicorn, "if you'll believe in me, I'll believe in you. Is that a bargain?"

—Lewis Carroll, *Through the Looking Glass*

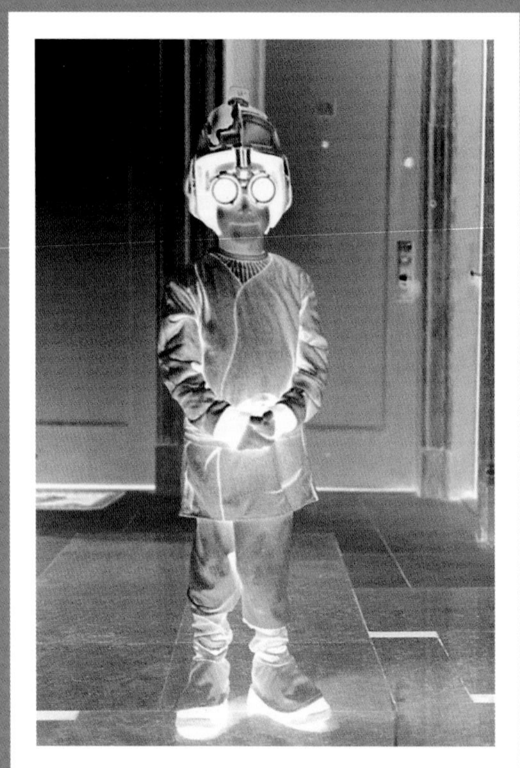

JABBERWOCKY

'Twas brillig, and the slithy toves
Did gyre and gimble in the wabe:
All mimsy were the borogroves,
And the mome raths outgrabe.

She puzzled over this for some time, but at last a bright thought struck her. 'Why, it's a looking-glass book, of course! And if I hold it up to a glass, the words will all go the right way again.'" Alice's bewilderment at seeing words in a mirror image in *Through the Looking Glass* is what looking at negatives made with a camera can be like. Disorienting but strangely revealing, it reminds us that a photograph—the output of that ubiquitous modern implement, the camera—offers us another way of looking at the world.

Using a camera allows us to see in Technicolor or black and white, rectangles or squares. It encourages us to observe our surroundings more acutely, to look beneath the surface of outward appearances.

While the camera transfers to film decisions that we make with our eyes, the resulting picture can surprise us, by capturing details, gestures, we did not notice when we released the shutter. Sometimes we look at a photo and experience more than what appears in print: the image of newly manicured grass brings back the smell of a freshly mown lawn.

Looking through the viewfinder teaches us to be more aware even when we are not taking pictures. When our senses are awakened, we notice the frothy sea water, the receding tide and fading footprints on the beach. New vistas open in our internal landscapes.

The camera imposes roles on picture-taker and subject. Photographers try to manipulate the situation, without seeming to. We say “smile for the camera” when we mean smile for us. We pretend we are not interested in taking a picture and then take one when our model least suspects. As subjects, children want to take our control away, and they do so quite well. They run off, turn their backs or deliver blank stares when we have asked for happy faces. We want the picture, so we can no longer make all the rules.

If the photographer is the parent and the subject is the child, conflict is often part of the scenario. Pursued by a camera, the child dominates the circumstances: the when, where, and how. It seems to be the child’s photograph, not ours. And yet the parent, by choosing the moment and the elements within it, determines the what, the ultimate image.

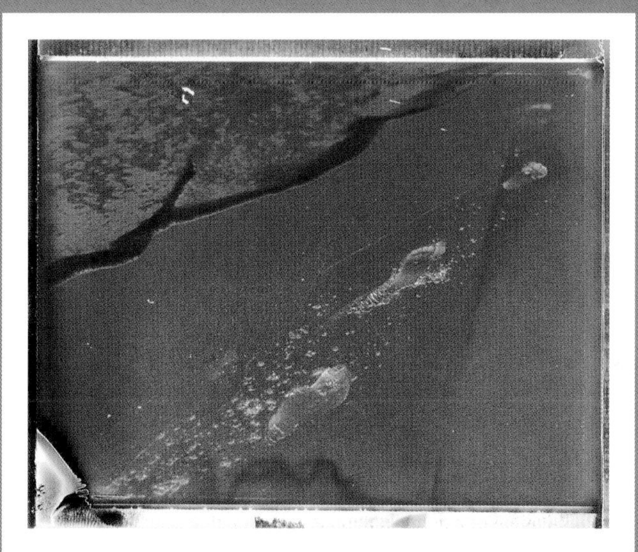

This little box exerts a lot of influence on our lives. It gives our children the power to be someone they might not otherwise have been: the prankster, the imposter, the athlete, or the beast. It gives us a fresh perspective on who our offspring really are. By recording the outcome of our interaction, the camera exposes hidden facets of our relationship. Both parent and child end up with something far more valuable than what they had intended or foreseen.

Once our camera relinquishes the recorded image to us, the photograph takes over. It remains fixed, while we are always changing. Years later, when looking at it again, we see it with altered recollections. Then the immutable photograph becomes the ever-renewing visual story of our lives.

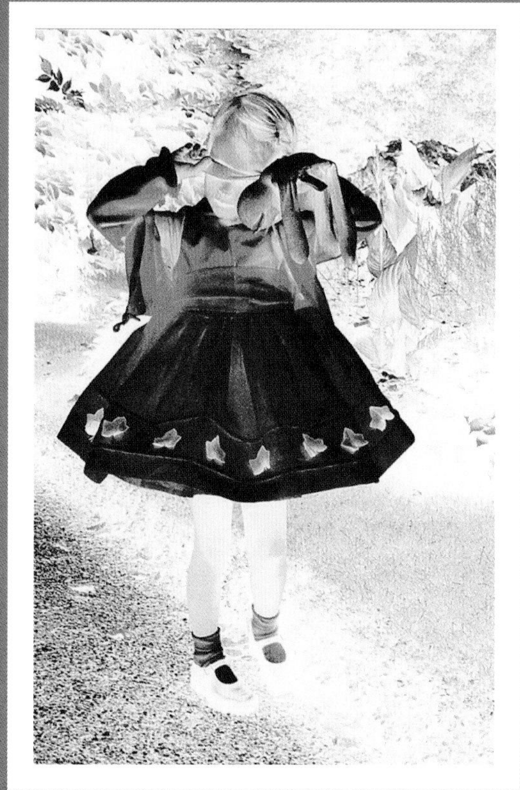

Jesse

jesse (jəs sé)
(noun): an original, one of a kind; consummate dealmaker; angel; scoundrel; (verb): demand, as in, "who made you the boss?"; (adj.): camerawise.

"If you think
we're wax-works,"
he said,
"you ought to
pay, you know.
Wax-works
weren't made to
be looked at for
nothing.
Nohow!"

—Lewis Carroll,
Through the Looking Glass

People
with
cameras
wear
me
out.

They
make
you
do
things
you
don't
want
to do,
like

stand up straight,
look at the camera
and
smile.

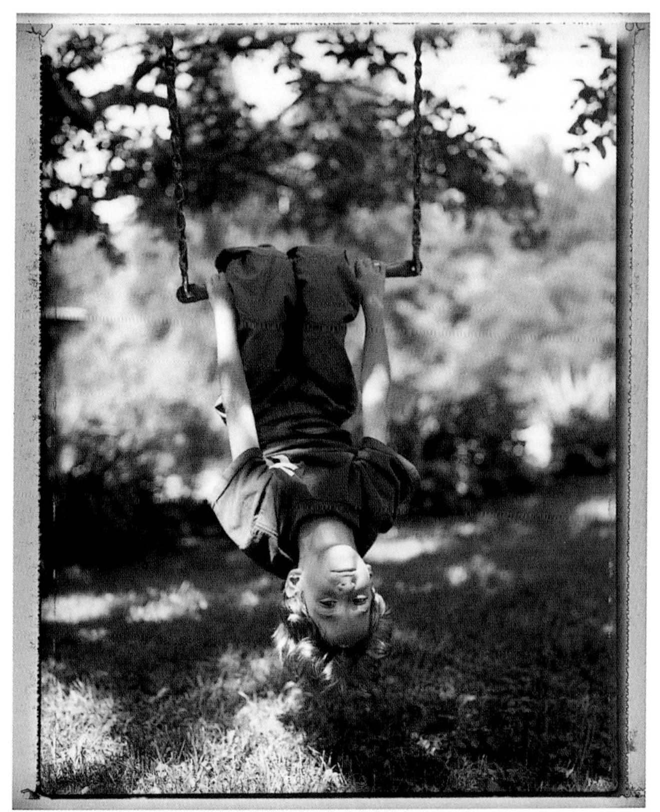

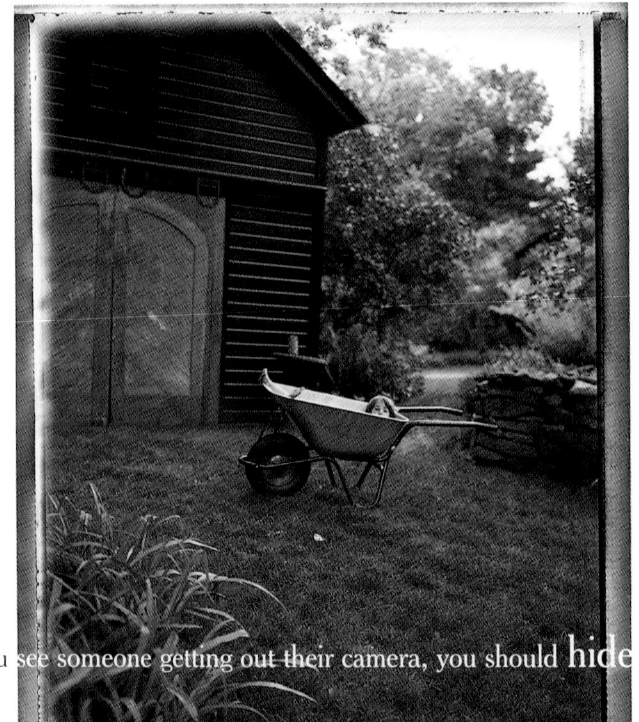

When you see someone getting out their camera, you should hide hide hide.

But here's the thing, it doesn't always work.

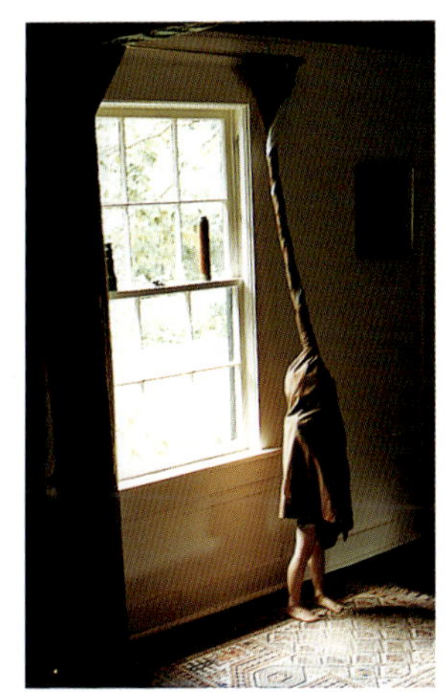

See

what

I

mean

?

My mom says
if you pretend something you don't like isn't there
it will

go away.

But she never does.

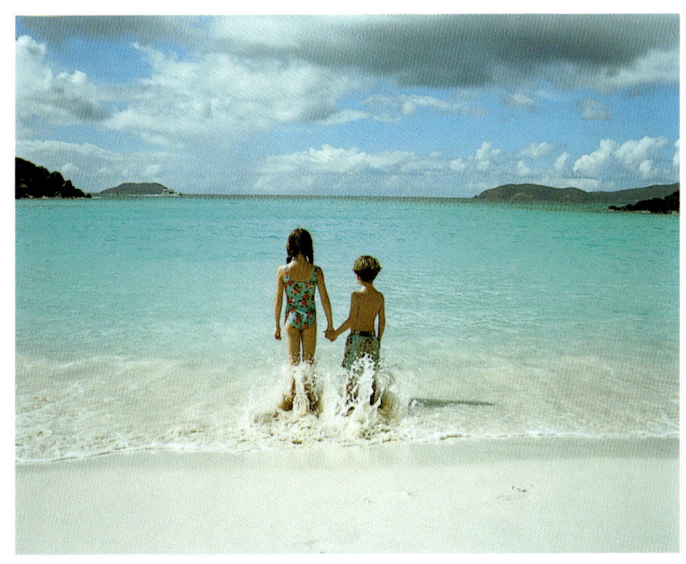

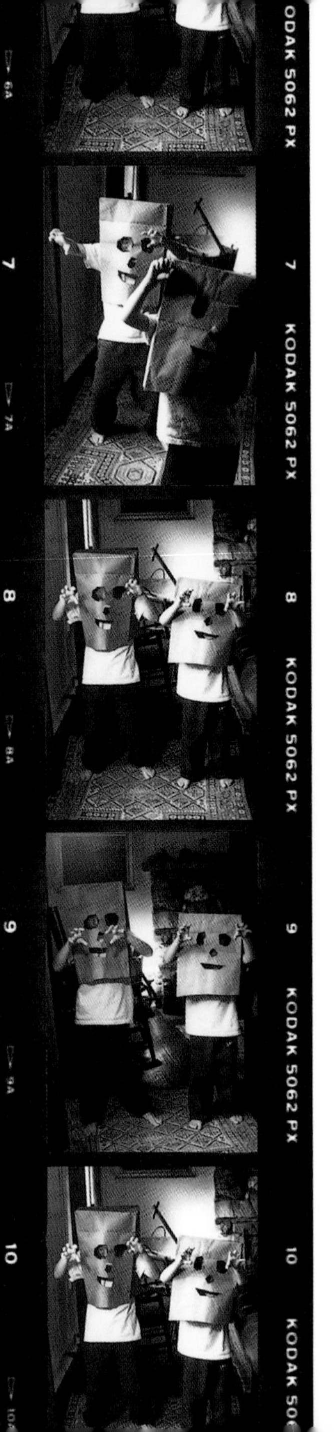

She

just

stands

there

and

takes

the

picture

anyway.

Click

click

click

click

•

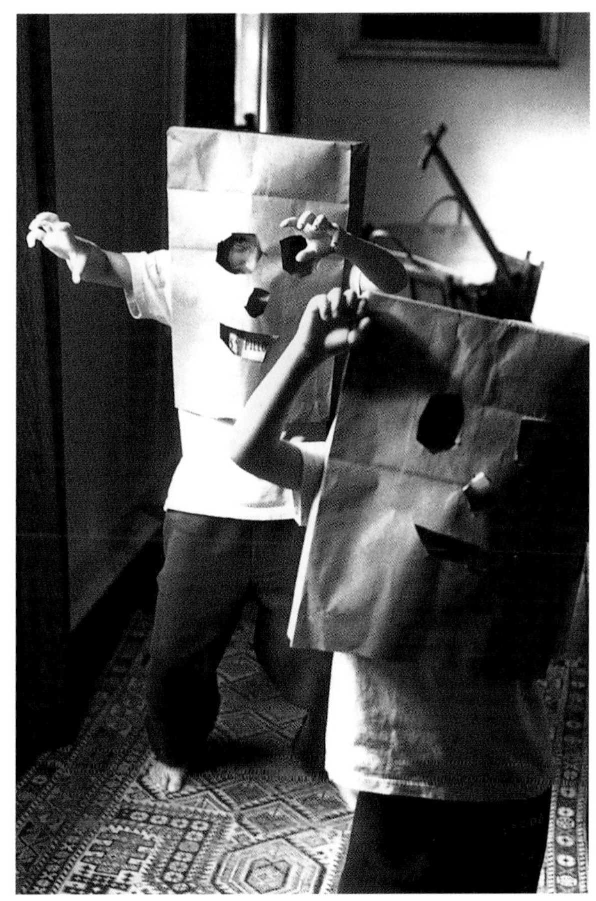

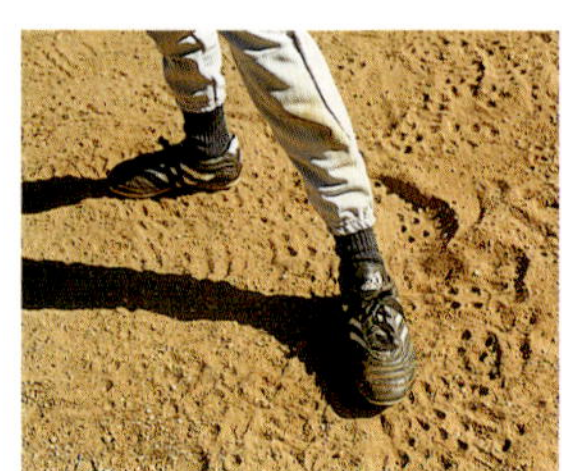

So then I put my best foot forward. “OK, Mom,” I say. “Let’s PLAY BALL.”

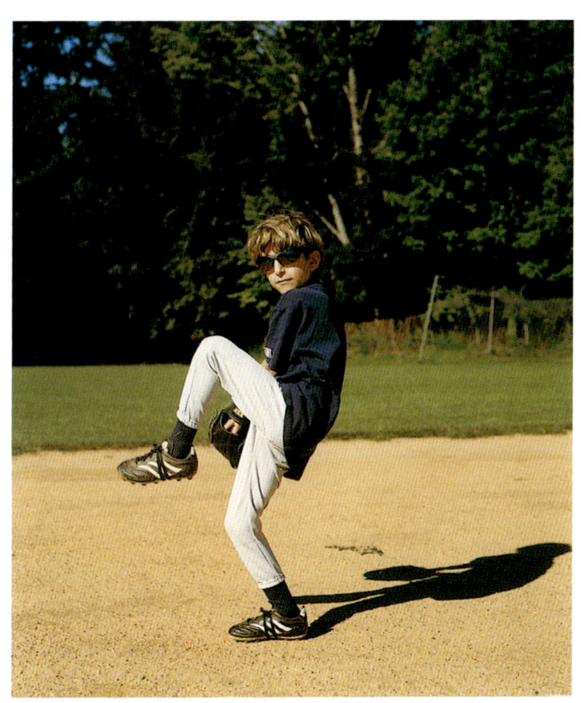

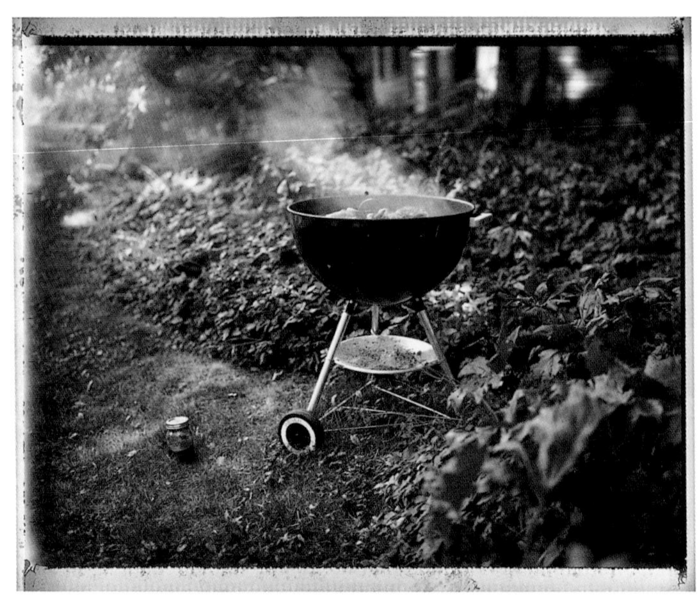

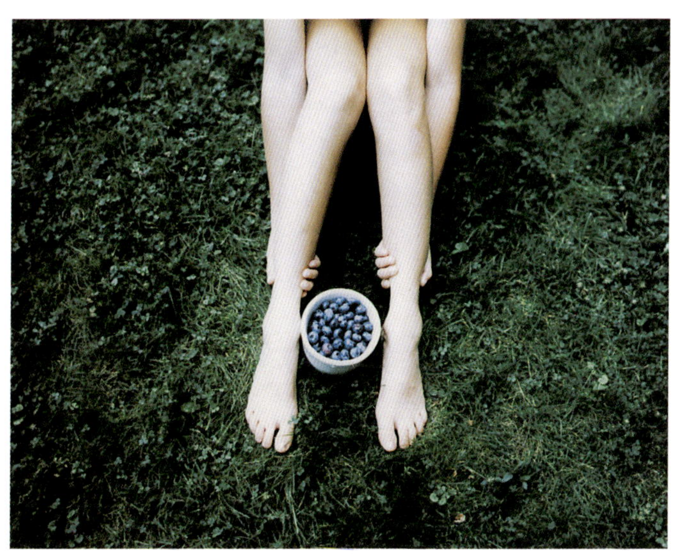

I take a better picture after I've had something good to eat.

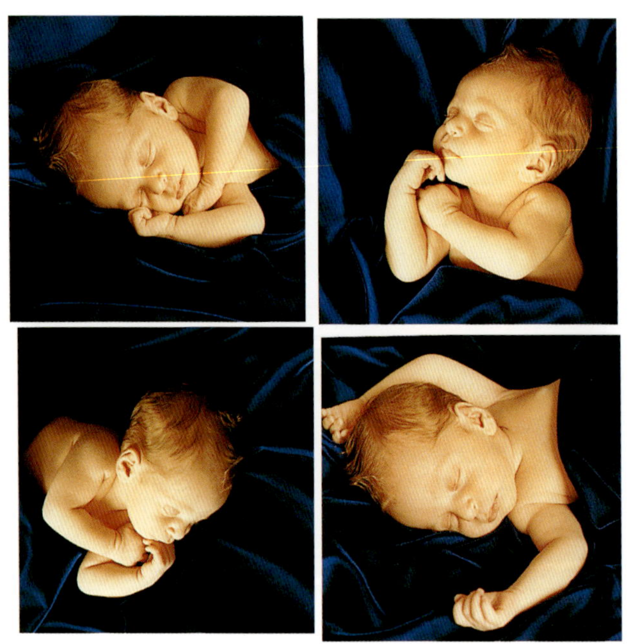

My mom says when I was a baby I was a very uncooperative subject. How much more cooperative can a baby be? She says having a baby was so much work. Looks to me like she spent an awful lot of time hanging around watching me sleep.

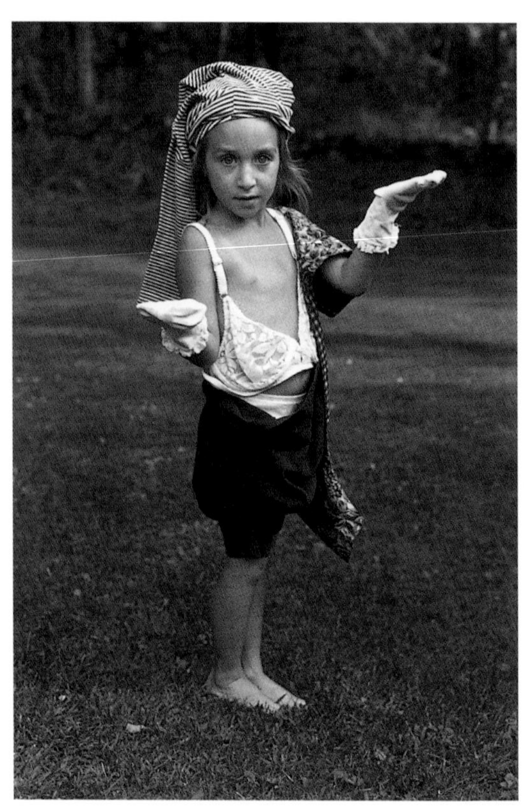

It isn't right for people to photograph kids doing things

they'd never in a million years be caught doing.

Once I tried to take a picture

of my mom without her shirt on. Boy, was that a mistake!

I like hanging out with these

guys having serious talks about mostly everything.

When that gets boring, we can always
kick our ball around, make lots of noise

and scare birds.

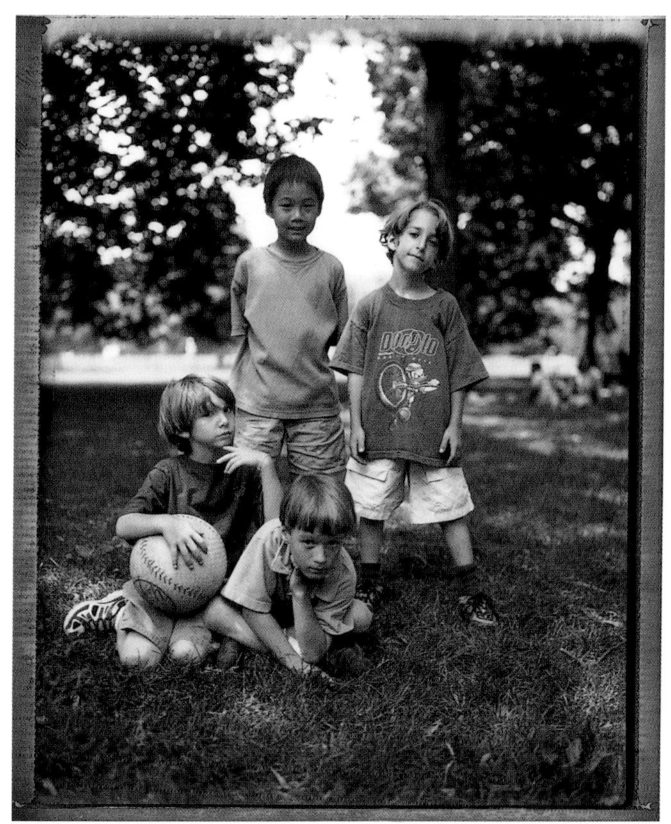

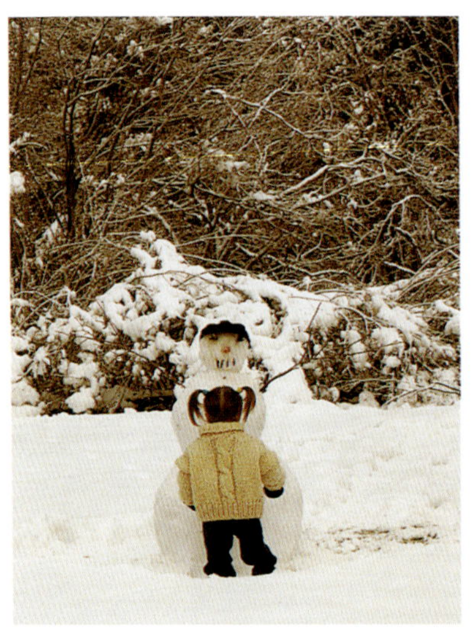

Picture people always try to get other people to loosen up. Hel-lo . . .

Hel-lo . . . How frozen is this guy's smile?

flying

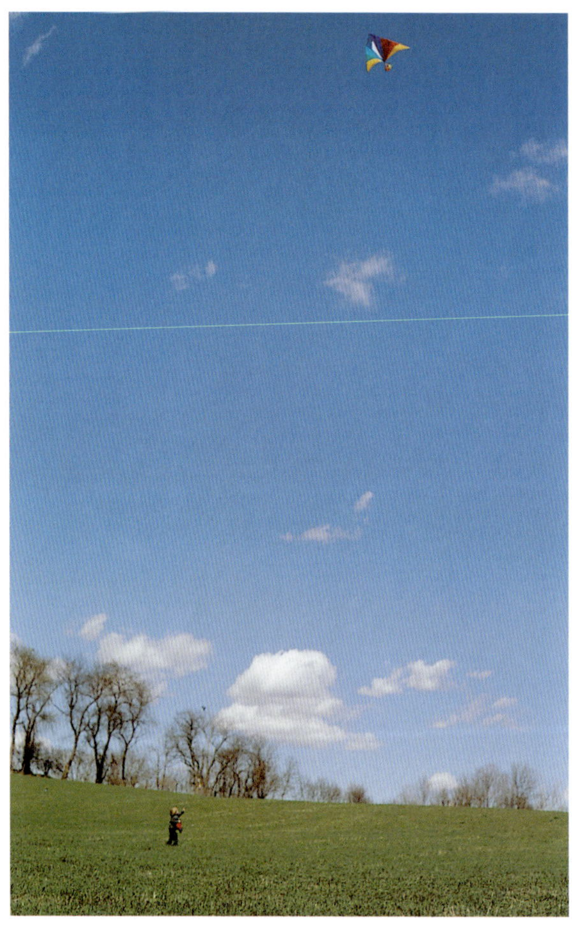

Here's something to remember: Grown-ups get really distracted by bright unidentified objects.

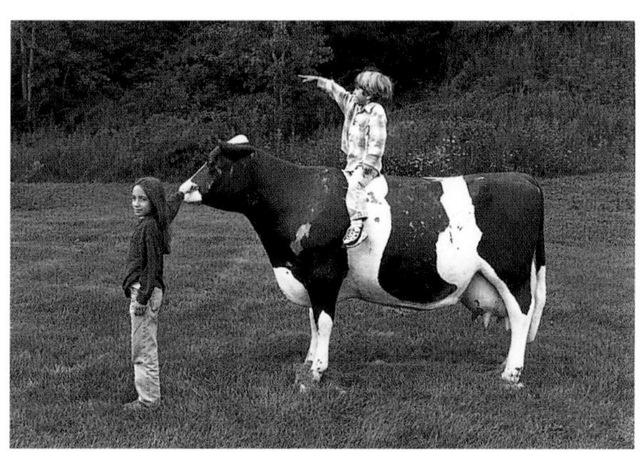

If there's no UFO, just pretend you see one.

Parents

love to

say,

"You can

be anything

you want

to be."

When I grow up,

I'm going to be

a world-class

tiger.

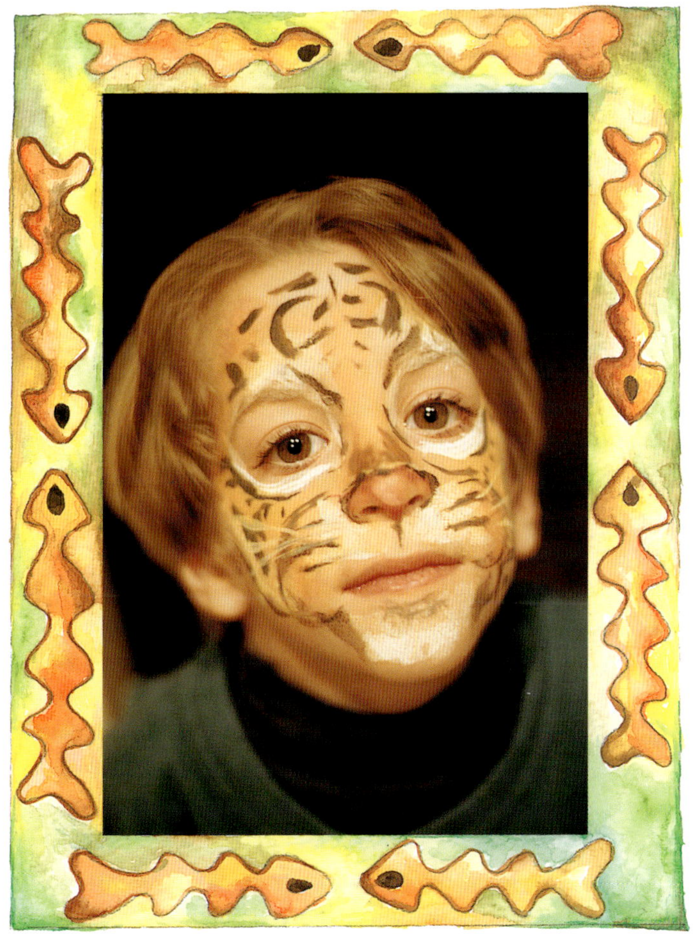

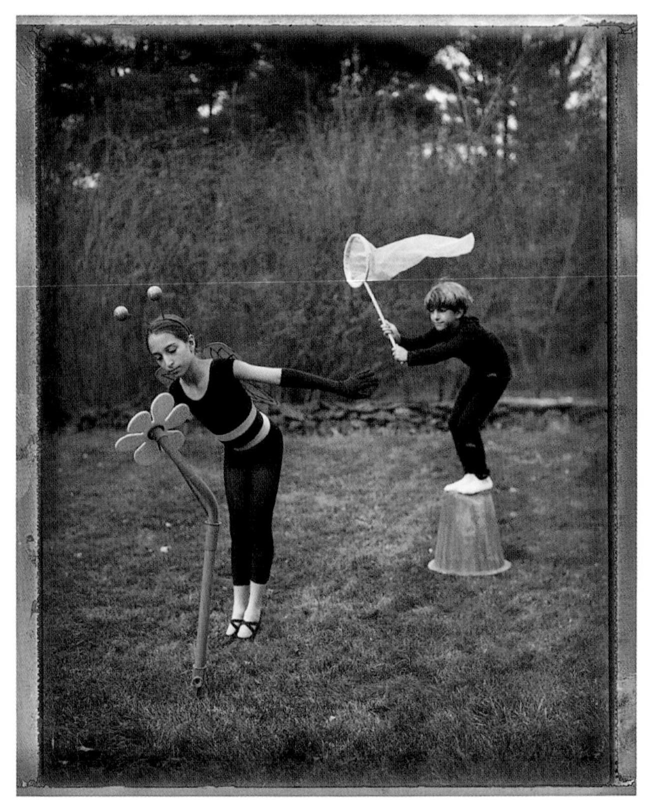

Maybe
I should grow wings, Then I'd zzzzzip
away so fast, nothing would catch   me.

Not even a shutterbug.

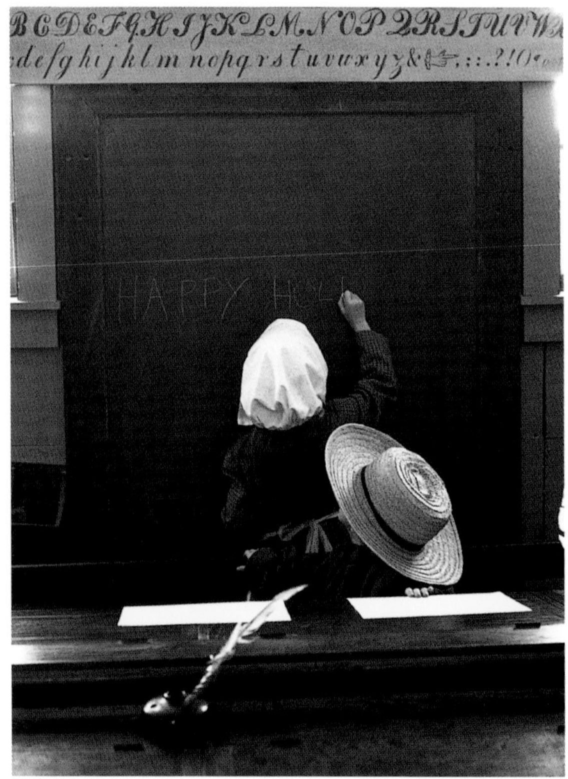

What's so HAPPY about the holidays?

More pictures. They

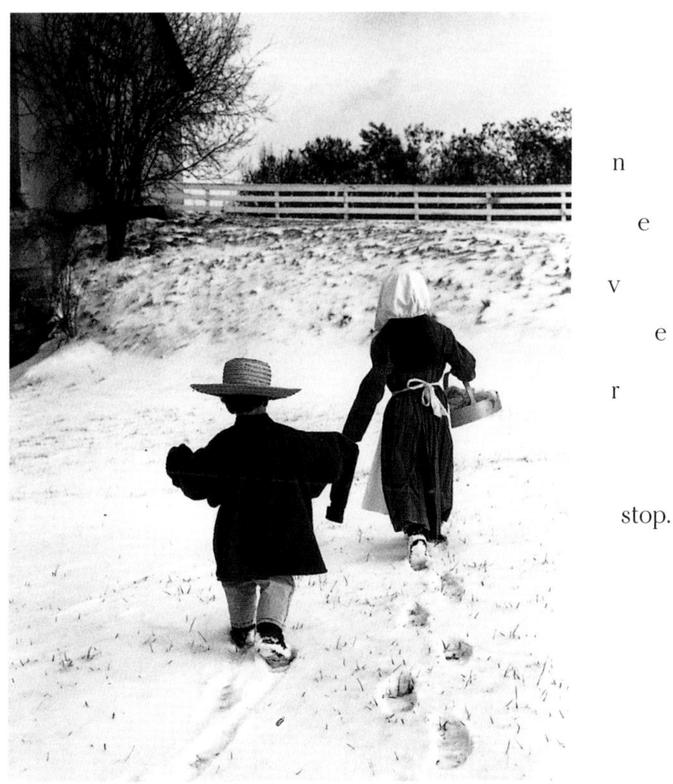

n
e
v
e
r

stop.

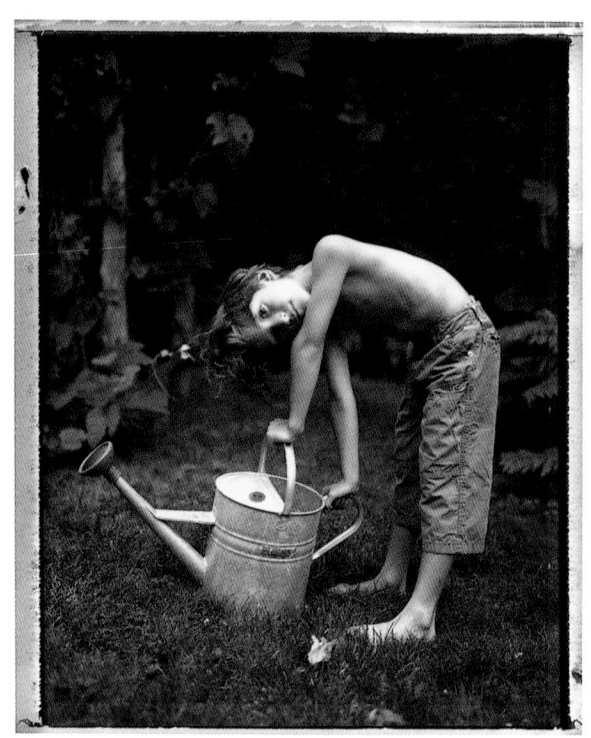

Some parents don't **ever** give their kids a day off.

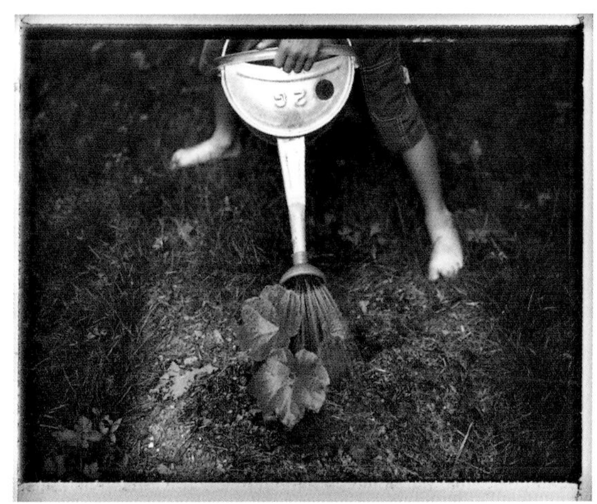

Sometimes I wish it would just rain.

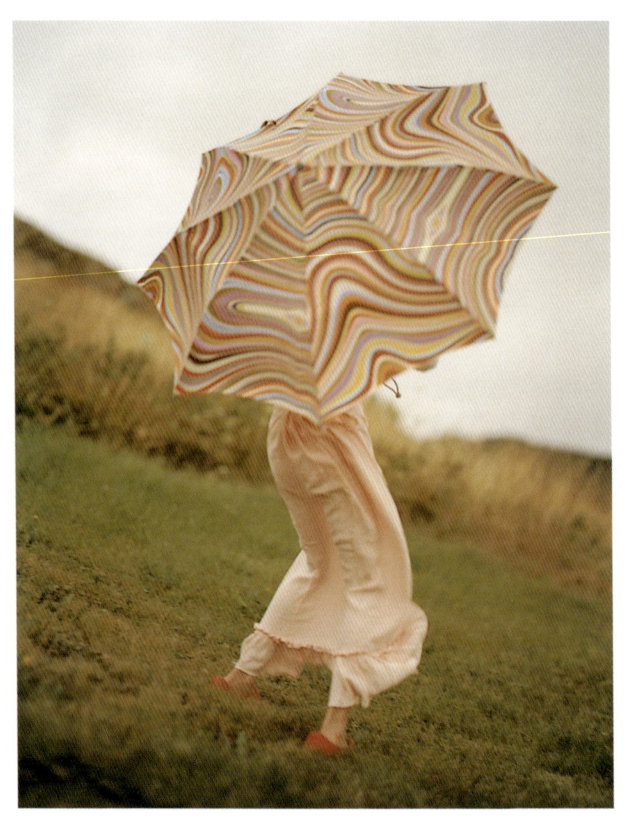

Of course, wind and rain and terrible storms won't stop my mom. She can really b l o w a person away. If it's my sister, I don't mind too much.

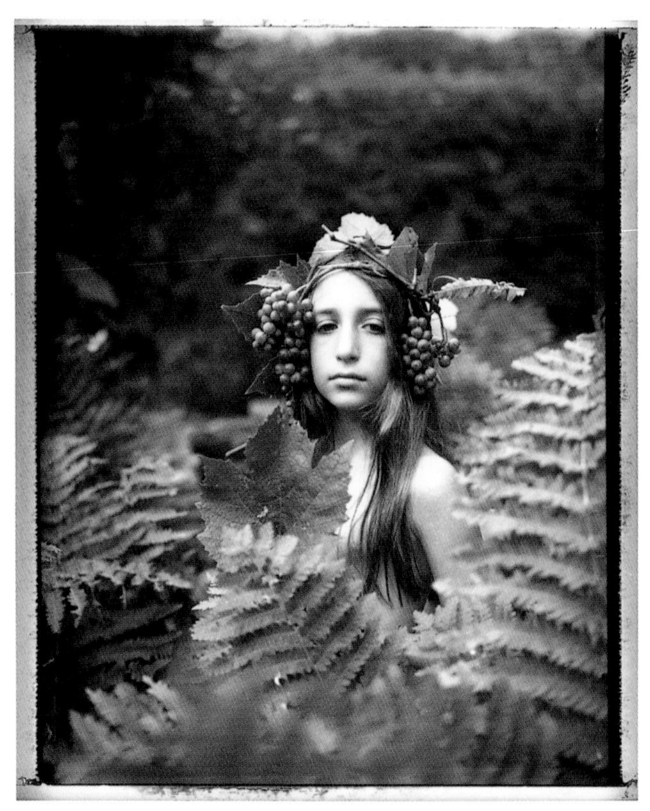

My sister will do anything my mom tells her to. You'd never catch

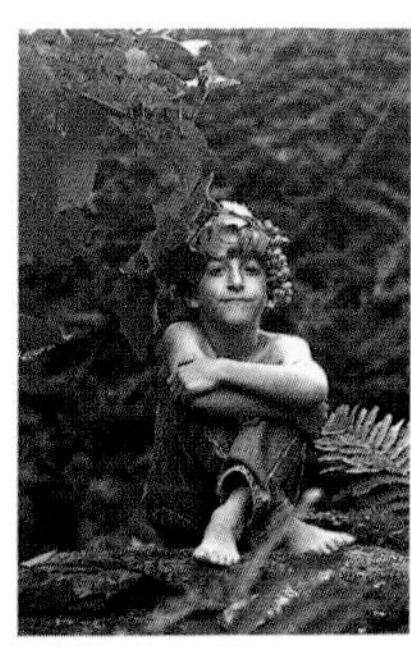

me wearing grapes on my head so some one can take a pic ture.

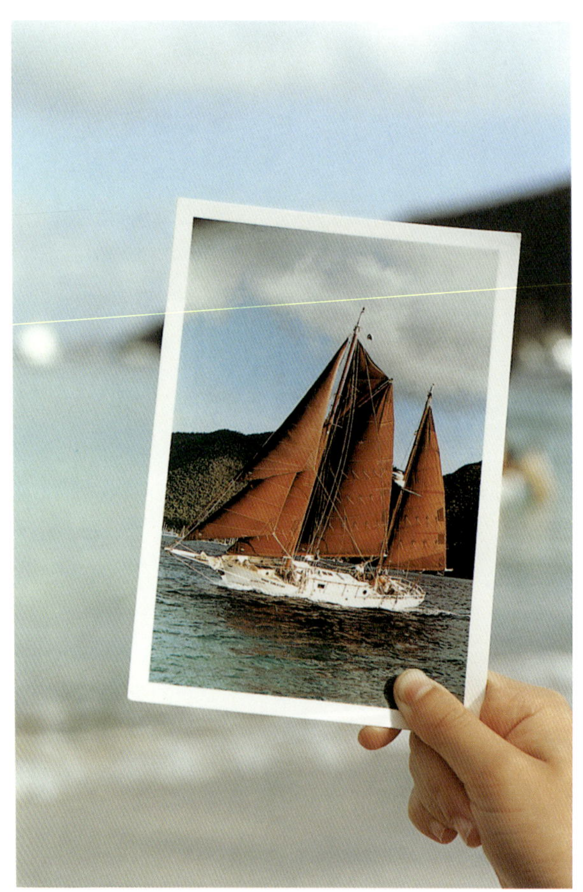

Lots of people go on vacation to have some fun.

I think my mom goes so she can take more pictures of me and my sister.

Once on a trip to the Caribbean, she brought so many cameras they stopped her in customs.

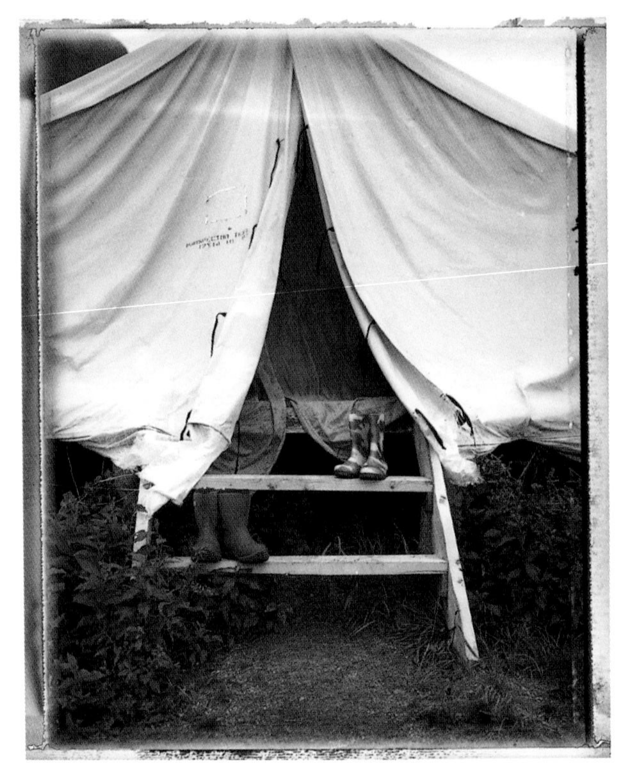

We went camping one summer. I found

a starfish. Good thing my mom had her camera.

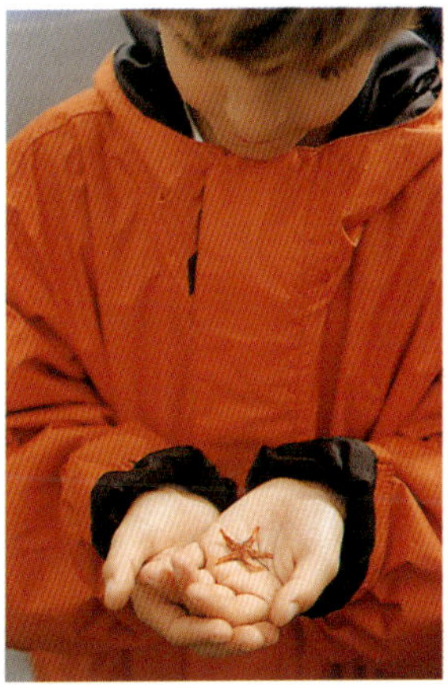

(Don't tell her I said that.)

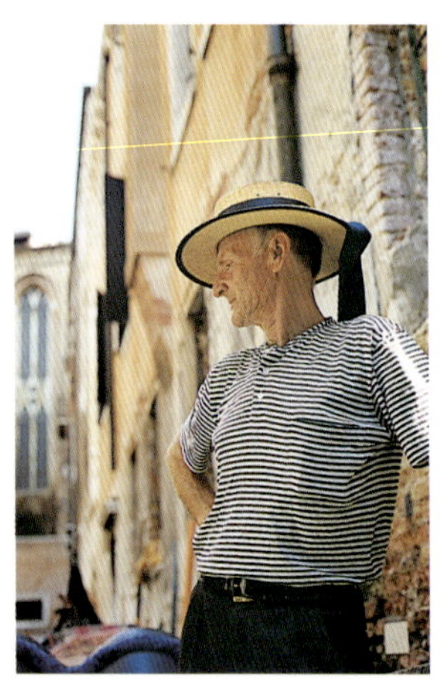

When we traveled in Venice, it was so great. We saw people and places we'd never seen before. My mom could even take pictures of someone other than me. When too many people were around, we had to get up with the **roosters** just so she could get her picture. At least we got to keep the masks.

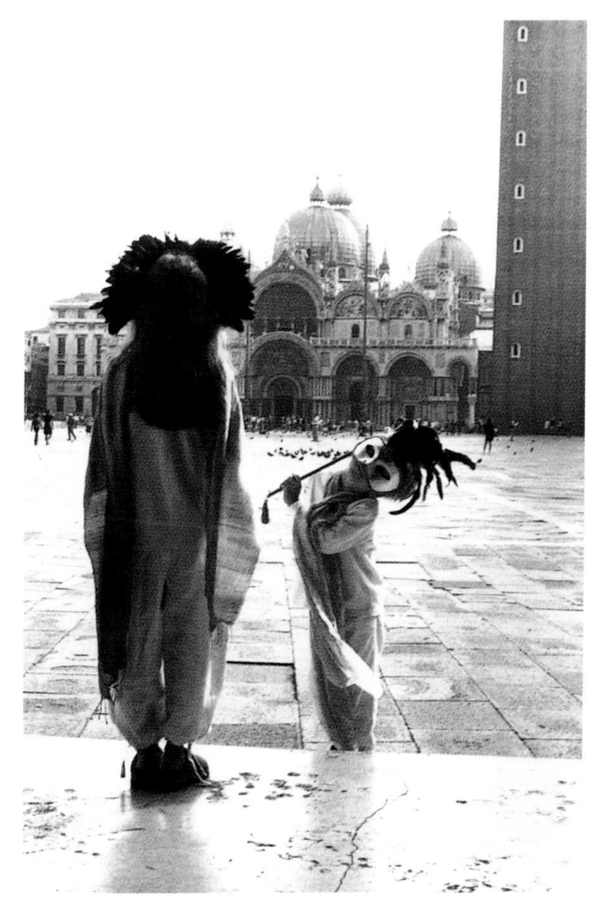

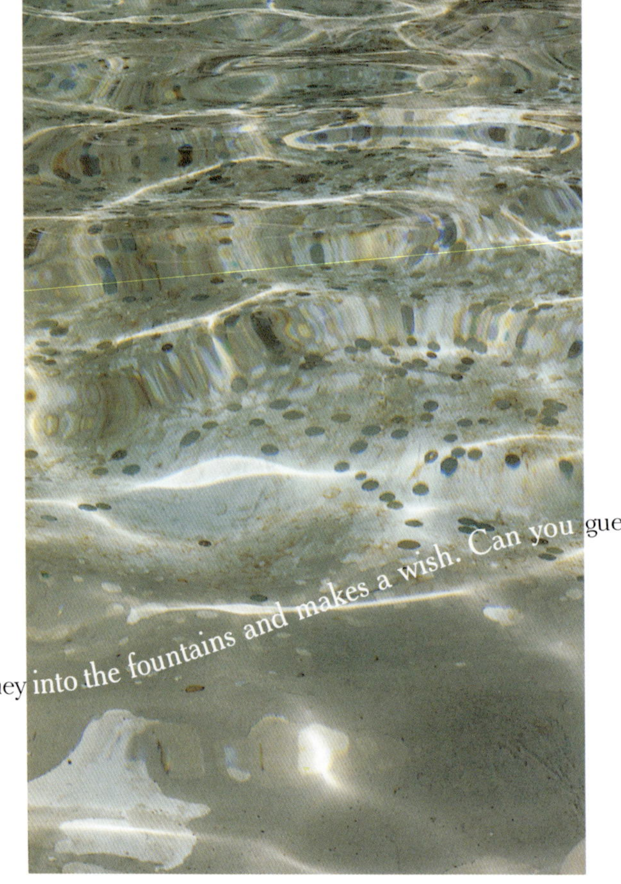

In Rome, everyone throws money into the fountains and makes a wish. Can you guess what mine was?

Maybe

I

should

have

bought

an

extra

wish.

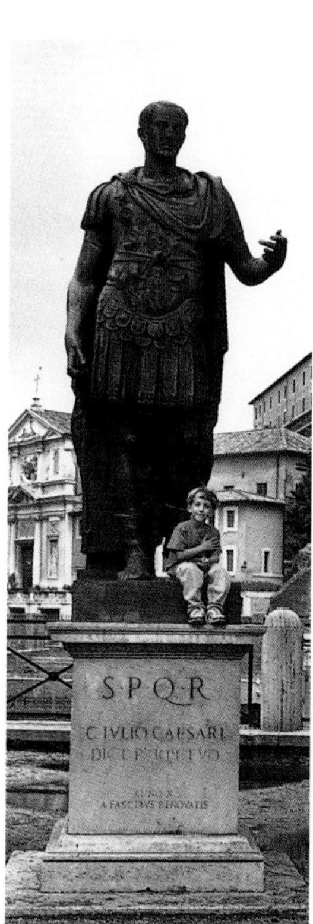

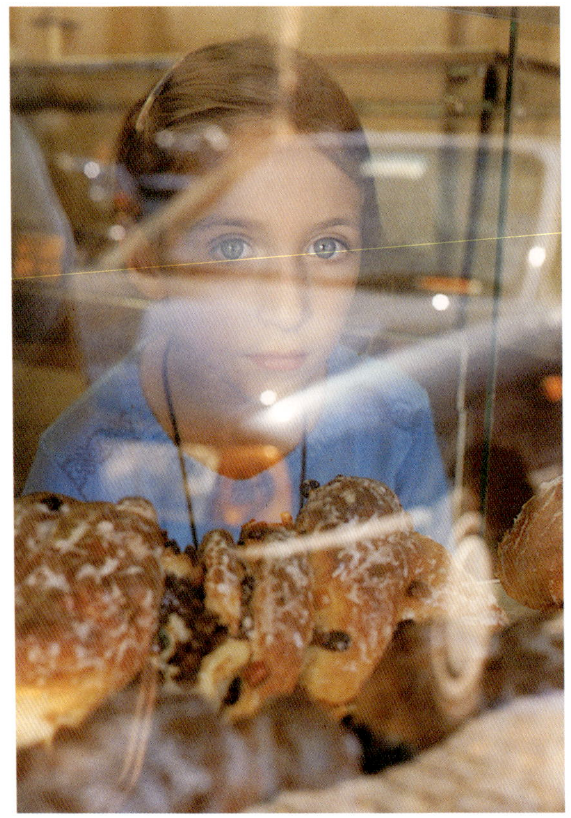

Italian food is good: mounds of pasta and sweets. It takes your mind off all those museums and ruins.

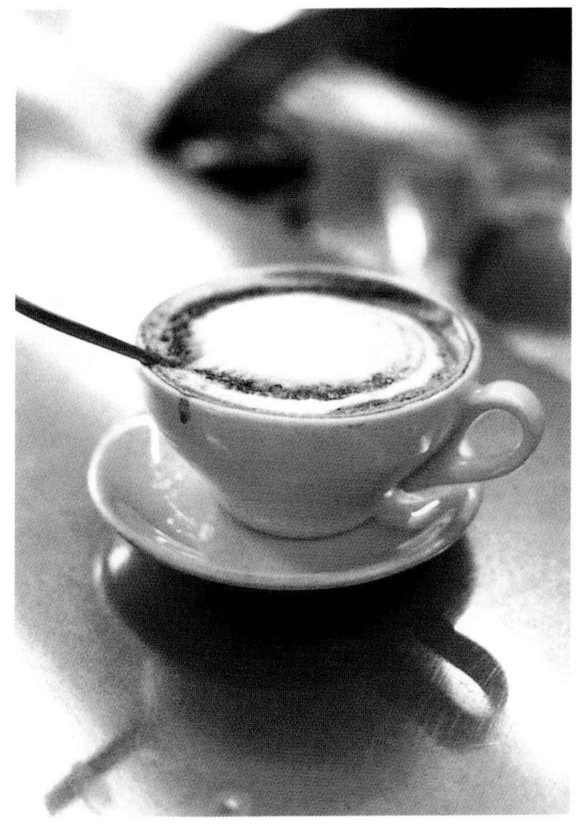

After a few little treats, nothing will bother you. Especially a bothersome camera person.

People say life is a game of give and take. Mostly I like taking.

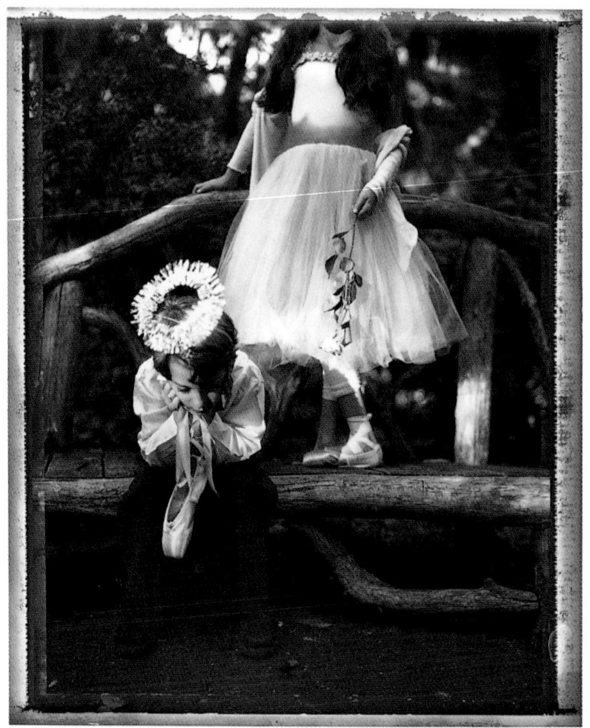

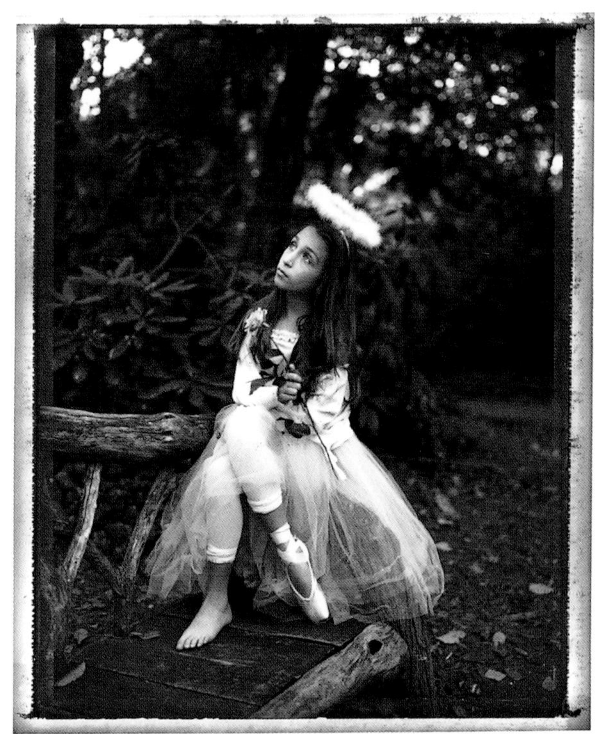

I can always give it back after the picture's done.

Let's all sing after me —

for I'm a jolly good fellow

for I'm a jolly good fellow

which nobody can deny.

for I'm a jolly good fe-el-low

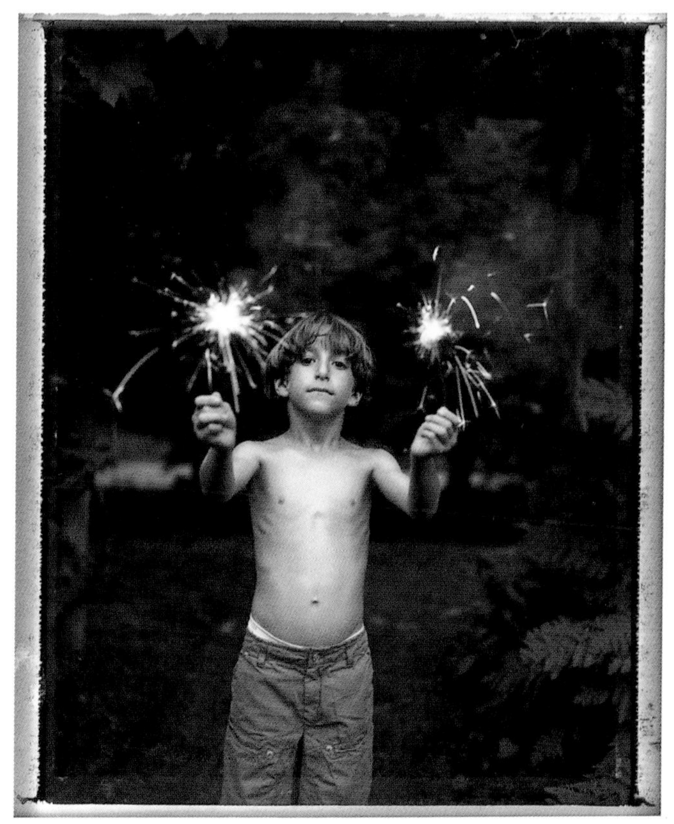

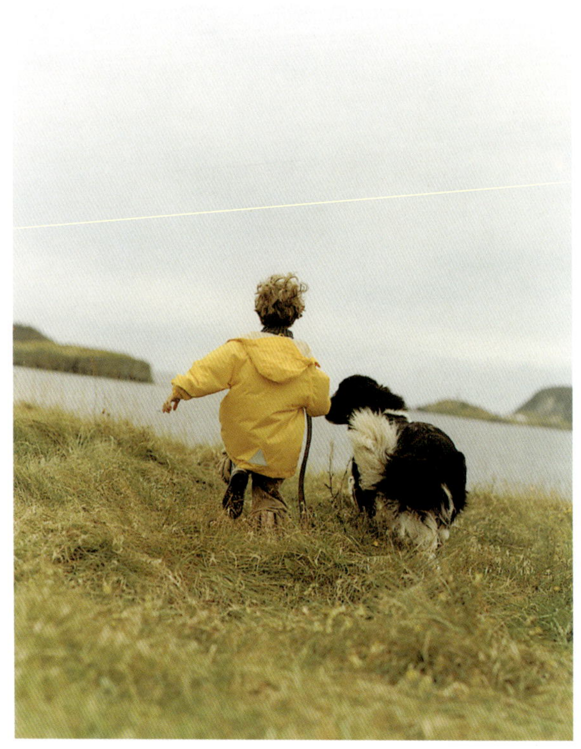

Free. At. Last.

The Photographer

photographer (fə tag´ rə fər)
(noun): person behind the camera; dream catcher; (verb): record; create; color; (adv.) persuasive; (adj.) powerful; powerless; obsessed.

"Years afterwards
she could bring
the whole scene
back again, as if it
had been only
yesterday."

—Lewis Carroll,
Through the Looking Glass

It took me a long time to think of myself as a photographer. I like simple things, and photography, I felt, employed so many gadgets, involved too many choices. Adrift in a sea of technology, I didn't know where to begin.

Initially, I owned a basic camera—manual with one lens—and I began taking the occasional, basic picture. After the birth of my first child, I reached for the camera more and more, and found myself becoming increasingly adventuresome. I tried different lenses, even different cameras. I photographed at all times of day, in many kinds of light. I rearranged objects and subjects, and experimented with composition. There were times when my picture was not working out. Then I put my camera down. Patience, I discovered, was the key to success.

Not knowing the rules worked to my advantage. Imperfection can give a photo spontaneity and life, making it a moment with a story as opposed to just a story without a moment. A picture is more rewarding when it captures how we feel about our subjects: the lost tooth, the new dress, the first snowman. It is the vision, the point of view, that makes the photographer.

Children often take great photographs. They respond with true emotion to what they see, without preconceptions. They crop off heads and take pictures of feet, torsos, hands. They don't ask people to look at the camera and say cheese; often their subjects are completely unaware that they are being photographed.

Imitating work that we like can help to develop a personal style. I began to copy my kids' approach. I found that body parts could tell a story as well as a head shot. A picture seen from the back could have as much impact as one from the front. I took pictures at odd times. Sometimes I'd even take one after the children had left the scene, to see if I could somehow catch their essence on film.

I know at times my family takes issue with me and my camera. They think I use up too much of their time, that my requests are unreasonable. A photographer is, by nature of the act, an intruder, an interloper, intolerably assertive. We must be: with a click we can immobilize the transitory, with a click we can record the fleeting. Once the moment has passed, nothing can bring it back.

• • • the other side of the picture

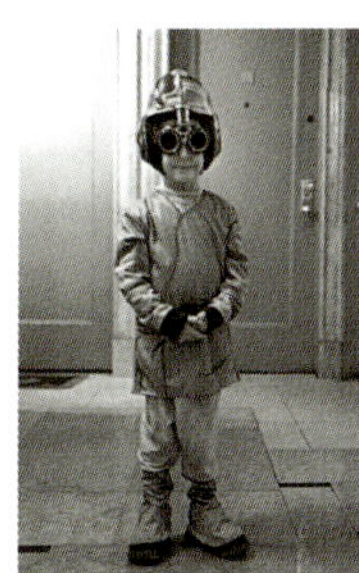

I love this photo. Jesse hates it.

I love that his Anakin costume was so big that it bunched and twisted around his ankles. He hates that the costume was so big that it made him look like a dork. I love the dim light, the black-and-white floor tiles, and the spacelike quality of the picture. He hates that he will be forever preserved in this unseemly fashion.

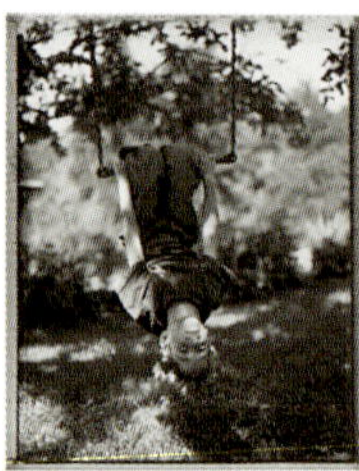

We were visiting friends in Vermont. A swing hung from a tree in their orchard. Pictures can reverse the way we see things. Kids will often look at the world upside down, inside out, backward and forward. I try to do the same.

The family got me a French wheelbarrow, guaranteed not to tip over. My son had to climb in to test it out. People don't usually think of everyday objects as photographic tools. Here the aluminum basin was the perfect reflector, illuminating Jesse's little face and feet. "Wait. Don't move," I instructed. Then I ran and got my camera.

We got off the plane in the Caribbean and couldn't believe the color of the water, the sky. I wanted to portray the island's tranquility. If the kids had been facing me, the picture would have been about them. I was looking for an image about their relationship to the place, to each other. When they turned their backs to me, I found it.

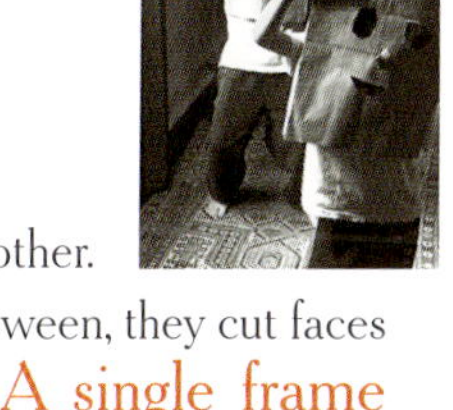

When my children aren't fighting, they will occasionally amuse each other. One afternoon, after a discussion about what they should be for Halloween, they cut faces into two paper bags and ran around the house trying to be scary. A single frame couldn't do the scene justice, so I photographed it as a sequence.

My son loves baseball. Not just the game, but all the stuff that goes along with it. Hours are spent in front of the mirror, perfecting the gesture, the stance, the look. I told him he was a picture of cool and he rewarded me with a photo op.

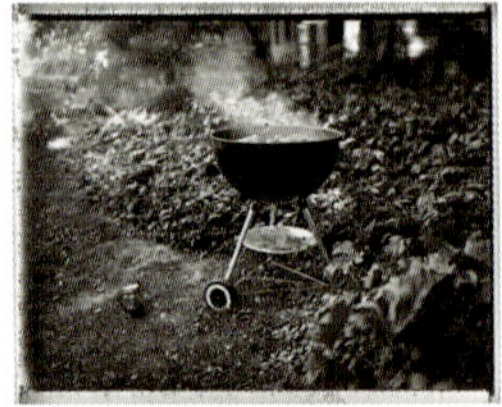

One Father's Day, we decided to go traditional. Since my husband already had plenty of ties, we thought a new outdoor grill was the perfect gift. Photographed on its own, without the children, it became an icon of American family life.

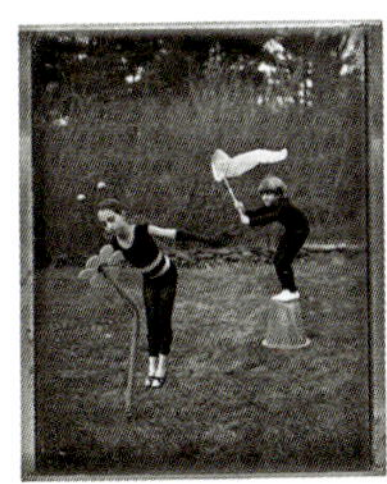

After I took one picture of this whimsical setup, I tried several variations and permutations, but found it hard to improve on my first attempt. The kids finally got fed up with me and walked off our little set. Sometimes it's best to leave well enough alone.

Getting a really good picture of my newborn was one of many great challenges I faced in the early days of motherhood. After numerous failures, I noticed that treated to a bath and feeding, my baby was in such a state of bliss, I could put him down by a sunny window and photograph him for two hours straight.

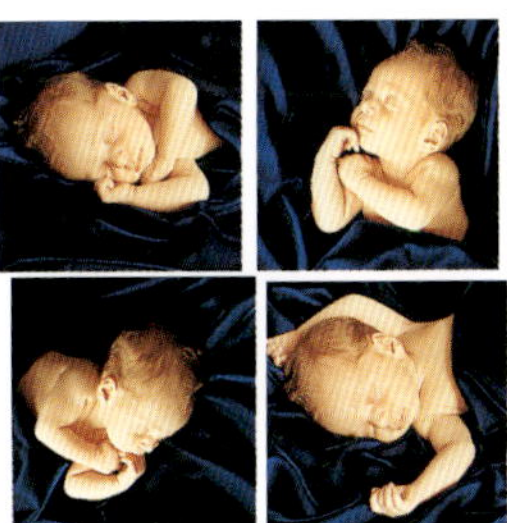

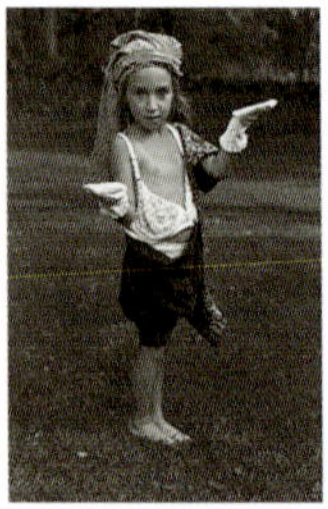

From an early age **my daughter discovered that dressing up was an activity that allowed her to defy convention.** She was particularly proud of this ensemble. I offered to record it for posterity, and she graciously accepted.

The first afternoon that summer was officially in play, I brought "the boys" to the park for an informal game of soccer. Following a round of running, kicking, and cheering, they paused—just long enough for me to take their picture.

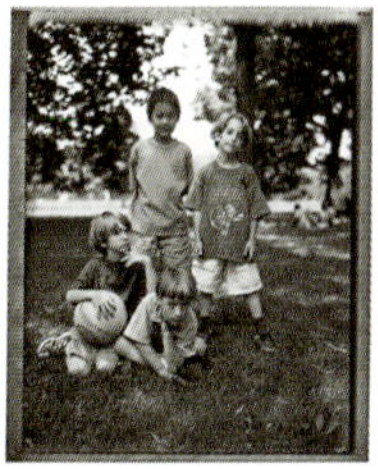

After the initial thrill of seeing a world sheathed in white, my daughter learned to make a man out of snow. Of course, she posed for the traditional child-and-snowman photo, but I found that I preferred this one, of her engaged in a silent dialogue with our creation.

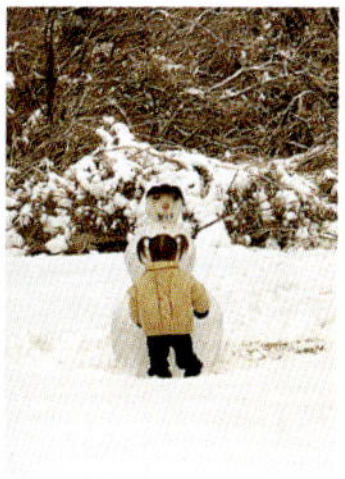

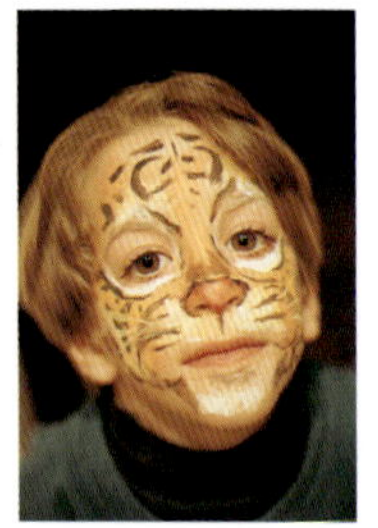

Often the simplest shots are the most rewarding. My son had gone to a friend's birthday party, where a book illustrator was painting the children's faces; Jesse chose to be a tiger. I love the sincerity of his expression.

Several times a year, we go to the Dutchess County Diner for the world's best three-berry pancakes and "he-man specials." The fiberglass cow stands outside and is always a big draw. I finally remembered to bring a camera on one of our visits and encouraged the children to do something funny. This is what they came up with.

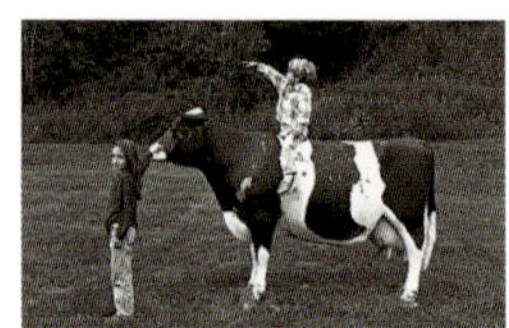

Each year it becomes an ever-mounting challenge to fashion a holiday card that will amuse family and friends. When a local historic village announced it was hosting a costume day, we seized the opportunity. I deliberately took the photograph before my daughter finished writing on the board. I felt it added tension and energy to the picture.

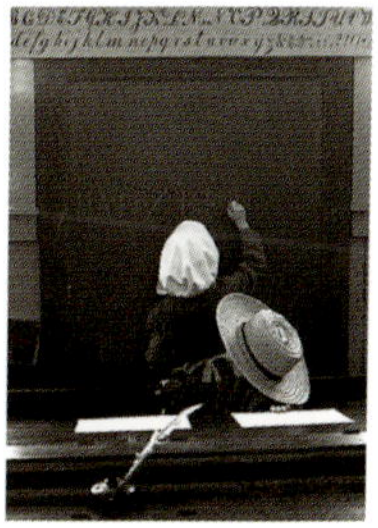

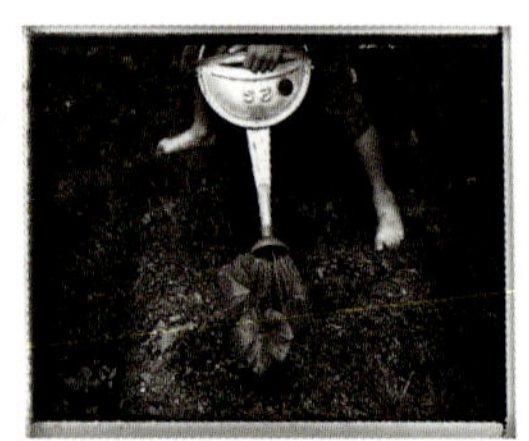

I wanted to capture my feelings about summer on film: with leaves of grass between our toes and the sun on our backs, we watered the garden and fed our souls.

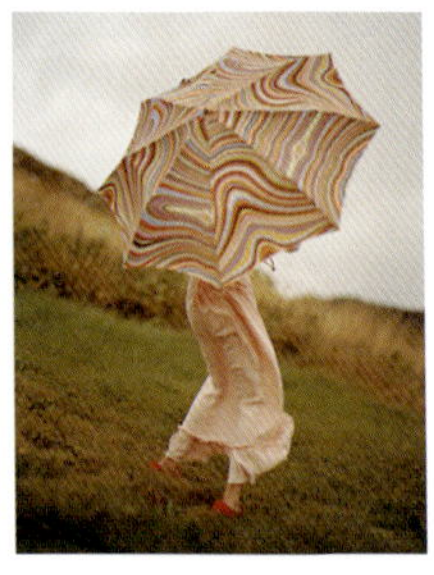

I saw my daughter standing on this hillside with her umbrella and felt called to action. I retrieved my camera, focused and aimed when a huge gust of wind came along and buckled her knees. Snap. I couldn't have planned it better.

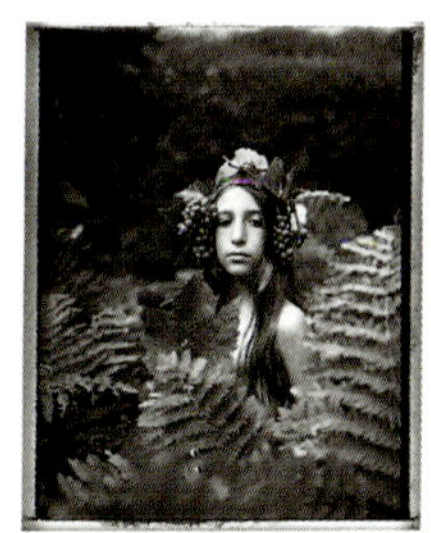

We had so much rainfall one spring, the trees and vines were dripping with fruit. To celebrate the harvest, we made grape wreaths. My daughter stood in the middle of some ferns. She looked like a figure in a Botticelli painting. I took the picture in black and white, to give the image a more classic feel.

Trips to exotic destinations can be exhausting. Everything is so beautiful, it's hard to process it all. I'm constantly whipping out my camera, determined not to miss a thing. Some days, it's a good idea to leave all the equipment behind and enjoy the vacation firsthand, rather than through the viewfinder.

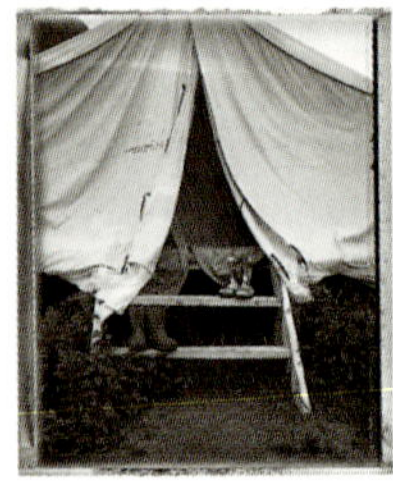

Our travels took us camping on the coast of Newfoundland, where the landscape is endlessly dramatic. Along with the obligatory scenic images, I found the more intimate vignettes equally appealing: the kids' boots outside our tent.

It's hard to take a bad picture in Venice. The kids were so hooked on all the costumes; we bought them each a feathered mask and silk scarf. They posed theatrically throughout the city's piazzas, attracting quite a crowd. Strangers stopped and asked to also photograph them.

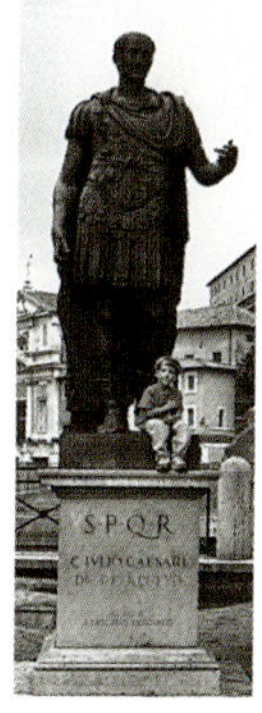

I've never understood why tourists feel the need to be photographed beside statues and artifacts. It's as though having the picture of the place isn't enough proof that one actually was there. But on one occasion I too succumbed. We came upon this huge statue of Caesar in the center of Rome and sat our tiny son at the base. "Hail, Caesar!" we commanded, and he obeyed.

Our family embraces the entire culture of new places we travel to. Along with the sights, we make sure to sample everything, at least once. **I try to keep a record of our best finds:** a perfect cappuccino in San Eustachio, the heavenly ricotta cake in the Jewish quarter.

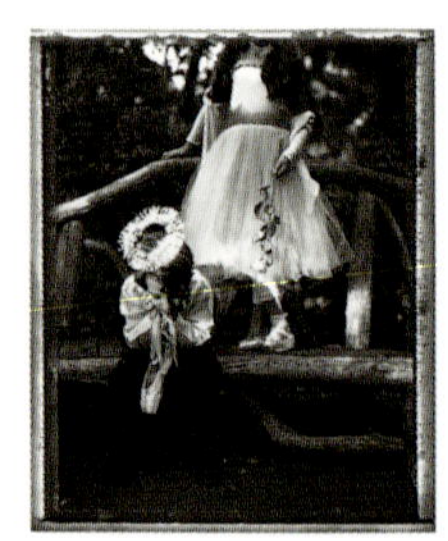

I imagined a fanciful photo of my two angelic children in the park. By the time we got to this spot, my son was tired, hungry, and bored. He grabbed his sister's slipper and moped. When I looked through the camera, I liked what I saw. This picture was actually more telling than the one I had envisioned.

We celebrate the Fourth with people, food, and flags. Jesse feels it is his patriotic duty to light up the night sky. For him, the holiday proclaims both our nation's independence and the freedom of summer. I was happily surprised by the contrast of his heroic pose and the energetic burst of the sparklers in this picture.

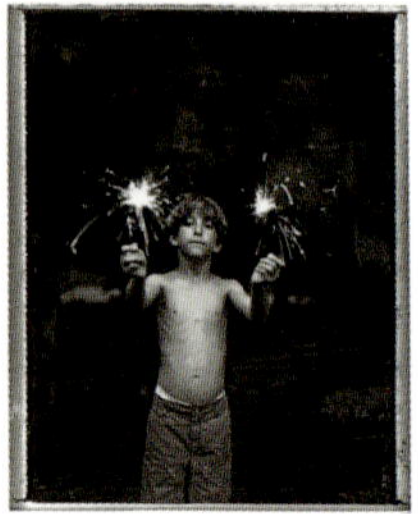

Dogs are my son's best friends. He met this one in Canada. After the two sniffed each other out, they turned, as if on cue, and tore through the tall grass. Even though I feel like I'm always toting my camera around, I seem to not have it at moments like these. Luckily, this time I did.

The authors would like to thank their families and friends for their encouragement and support during the writing of this book, especially Robert Dembo, Edmund Day, and Pat Bates. For their belief in the project and work to make it a success, we are indebted to our agent, Liz Darhansoff, and to our editor, Suzanne O'Neill. Our thanks also to Lissa Margulies of APM Darkrooms, New York City, for her masterful printing of the black-and-white photographs; to BSPL, New York City, for the color printing; and to Deborah Rust for her technical help.

Acknowledgments

"Why, you're only a sort of thing in his dream!"—Tweedledee to Alice
Through the Looking Glass, Lewis Carroll

3D are Hadas Dembo, Sandra DiPasqua, and Carol Olsen Day. This is their first book together. Hadas Dembo is a photographer and writer in New York. Her work has appeared in numerous publications, including *Travel & Leisure, Outside,* and *The New York Times*. In addition, she has produced photography for *National Geographic, Life, Newsweek* and Hyperion, among others. She has a degree in English Literature from Yale University and attended the International Center of Photography. She and her husband have two much-photographed children. Sandra DiPasqua is a senior art director at *The New York Times* and has been design and art director for Time Inc., Hearst, and Dow Jones. Her previous books include *Novena: The Power of Prayer* and *Holy Places,* published by Penguin Putnam. She lives in New York City with her family. Carol Olsen Day has been a writer-editor-producer for AOL Time-Warner, New Line Cinema, Time Inc., Hearst, and *Newsweek*. Her profiles of actors, directors, and artists have appeared in *People* and *Flair,* and she has also written and edited books for Simon & Schuster and G. P. Putnam's Sons. She works at *The New York Times* and lives with her husband in New York City.

About the Authors

The End